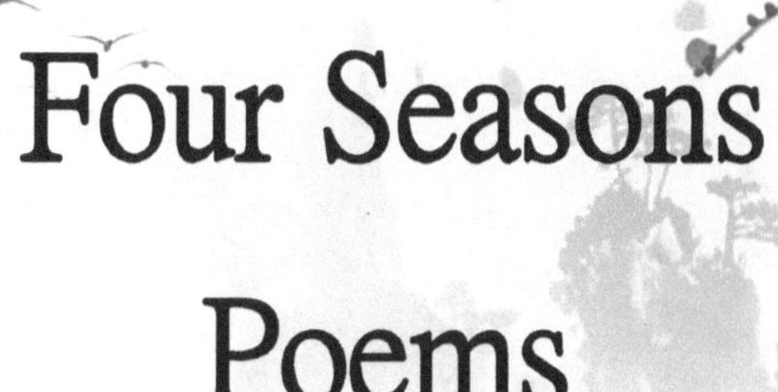

Four Seasons Poems

Author

LI ZHENJIN

ISBN:9798847830775

Preface

This collection of poems divides the year into 4 seasons and 24 solar terms by combining the ancient Chinese lunar calendar. In each solar term, the climate change and folk customs of the solar term are beautifully expressed through three ancient poems.

The author of this book, LI ZHEN JIN, a modern poet, has created many non-fiction novels and fantasy novels. His poems have Tang Dynasty style, and he is known as China's "Tang Dynasty Poet" in the 21st century and "Bai Juyi in the new century". His poems are deeply loved by the people. Poetry view: Poetry is the torch in the poet's heart, shining in the heart all the time.

In order to maintain the best respect for the poetry, we have only translated the introductory part of the poetry collection, and the ancient poetry part is still presented in Chinese. To appreciate the beauty of Chinese poetry, you need to have a certain foundation in Chinese.

Directory

The twenty-four solar terms------5
The Lichun------6
The Rain------10
The Jing Zhe------14
The vernal equinox------18
The Qingming Festival------22
The Grain Rain------26
The Lixia------30
The Xiaoman------34
The awn seed------38
The summer solstice------42
The xiaoshu------46
The Great Heat------50
The beginning of autumn------54
The end of summer------58
The Bailu------62
The autumnal equinox------66
The Cold Dew------70
The Frostfall------74
The beginning of winter------78
The Xiaoxue------82
The winter solstice------86
The Xiaohan------90
The Dahan------94

The twenty-four solar terms

The solar terms refer to the twenty-four seasons and climates. It is a supplementary calendar established in ancient China to guide agricultural affairs.

Since ancient China was an agricultural society, agriculture required a strict understanding of the operation of the sun, and farming was carried out entirely according to the sun, so the "24 solar terms", which reflected the cycle of the sun alone, were added to the calendar as the standard for determining the intercalary month.

The 24 solar terms of Chinese orthodoxy are based on Henan. The Chinese lunar calendar is a yin-yang calendar, that is, it is formulated according to the movement of the sun and the moon, so adding the twenty-four solar terms can better reflect the cycle of the sun's movement.

The Lichun

Lichun is the first solar term in the twenty-four solar terms. It is classified as the first month solar term in the official almanac of the Ming and Qing Dynasties; the arrival time is on February 3-5 every year in the Gregorian calendar (around the first day of the first month of the lunar calendar), when the sun reaches 315 of the Yellow Longitude ° hours.

Lichun is one of the important traditional festivals of the Han people. "Li" means "beginning". Since the Qin Dynasty, China has always started the spring with the beginning of spring. The beginning of spring is divided from the astronomical point of view, spring is warm, the birds and flowers are fragrant; spring is growth, sowing and sowing. The period from the beginning of the Spring Festival to the beginning of the summer is called spring.

立春*北京

轻风吹雨寒雪去，

一片飞花香自来。

今日春来浑不觉，

却将冬去问梅奴。

立春*上海

鹊去燕来不见岁，

一时相对两三里。

昨日梅花伴我眠，

今朝已是百花诞。

立春*桂林

寒风吹不休，

雪雨自相投。

莫念严冬景，

速迎一片春。

The Rain

Rain is the second solar term in the twenty-four solar terms, and it is located around the fifteenth day of the first lunar month (February 18-20 of the Gregorian calendar). The sun is at 330° ecliptic longitude. Indicates the beginning of precipitation and the gradual increase in rainfall. Let me take you to learn about the rainy season.

Rain indicates the beginning of precipitation and the gradual increase in rainfall. Rain has two meanings, one is that the weather is getting warmer, and the amount of precipitation is gradually increasing, and the other is that in terms of the form of precipitation, the snow is getting less and the rain is getting more and more. "The Seventy-two Hours of the Moon Order" said: "In the first month, the sky is full of water. The beginning of spring belongs to wood, but the one that grows wood must be water, so the rain after the beginning of spring. And the east wind is thawed, and it will be scattered and become rain. That's it."

雨 水*玉林

一树雨林洗愁眸，

半世云烟半世鸣。

常叹春光无限好，

却是春雨润前头。

雨水*玉林

水画春风迹，

色藏天地间。

一片清如洗，

千山翠万年。

雨水*海口

新枝抽芽新雨洗，

春花开来春草伴。

啼鸟声声向人和，

柳絮飘飘舞盛世。

The Jing Zhe

On March 5th or 6th every year, when the sun reaches 345 degrees of the ecliptic longitude, the solar term of "Jing Zhe" occurs. Sting means to hide. In the twenty-four solar terms, Jing Zhe reflects the growth and development of natural organisms affected by climate change.

A month after Jing Zhe started spring, the spring thunder began to sound. Animals and insects that have been dormant for the winter have ended their hibernation at this time and are ready to move. For example, Tao Yuanming once wrote a poem: "Promote the spring and choose the rain, the first thunder strikes the east corner, all the stings are lurking, and the vegetation is vertical and horizontal." In fact, insects can't hear thunder, and the earth rejuvenates and the weather warms. What brings them out of hibernation.

惊蛰*玉林

惊鹊鸣鸡噪，

飞萤落鸟影。

幽人知不见，

回首望山顶。

惊蛰*玉林

春雨润山川，

飞花新万里。

一声惊梦归，

万物始生长。

惊蛰*甘肃

一声雷鼓威仪地，

万里春风吹战尘。

千军万马齐呼应，

人勤农忙造丰年。

The vernal equinox

The vernal equinox, also known as "day in the middle", "day and night", and "mid-spring moon" in ancient times, meets around March 21 (20-22) every year, and the lunar calendar date is not fixed, when the sun arrives Yellow longitude 0° . According to "The Collection of the Seventy-two Hours of the Moon Order": "In the middle of the second month, it is divided into half, and this is half of the ninety days, so it is called the division." Another "Spring and Autumn Dew: Yin and Yang In and Out Chapters" says: " The vernal equinox is equal to yin and yang, so day and night are equal, and cold and summer are equal." There is a "Ming History Li Yi" that says: "The division is the point where the yellow and red intersect, and the sun travels here, and the day and night are equally divided." Therefore, the meaning of the vernal equinox, One is that day and night are divided equally, each of 12 hours; the other is that in ancient times, spring was from the beginning of spring to the beginning of summer, and the vernal equinox was in the three months of spring, which divided the spring equally.

春分*北京

微风吹雨分明月，

俏雪连夜奔西北。

尽得花香不见花，

却是梨花把春藏。

春分*北京

花落人间总不留，

水上云飞雪未休。

只恐东君归去头，

他日相逢又是秋。

春分*江苏

春色满江南，

窗外一枝香。

莫教梅梨分，

恐伤众芳娇。

The Qingming Festival

Qingming Festival, also known as Outing Festival, Xingqing Festival, March Festival, Ancestor Worship Festival, etc., falls between mid-spring and late-spring. The Qingming Festival originated from the ancestral beliefs and spring sacrifice rituals in ancient times. It is the most grand and grand ancestor worship festival in the Chinese nation. Tomb-sweeping Day has both natural and humanistic connotations. It is not only a natural solar term, but also a traditional festival. Tomb-sweeping, ancestor worship and green outing are the two major etiquette themes of Qingming Festival. These two traditional etiquette themes have been passed down in China since ancient times and have not stopped.

清明*上山

清明不见百花娇，

携路满眼春风雨。

莫恨江南无限思，

只今白发老人情。

清明*在山中

清晓人间一片梦，
不知何处是春种。
只今独立孤芳树，
却向山中见此共。

清明*下山

山下清明无一事,

人间万古有三生。

不知何处能留迹,

只恐当时已茫然。

The Grain Rain

Grain Rain is the sixth solar term of the twenty-four solar terms and the last solar term in spring. Dou refers to Chen; the ecliptic longitude of the sun is 30° ; it meets on April 19-21 of the Gregorian calendar every year. Grain rain means "rain gives birth to hundreds of grains". At this time, the precipitation increases significantly. The first seedlings and new crops in the fields need the moisture of rain. As the saying goes, "spring rain is as expensive as oil". With adequate and timely rainfall, cereal crops can thrive. Grain Rain, like the solar terms such as rain, small full, light snow, and heavy snow, is a solar term that reflects the phenomenon of precipitation, and it is the reflection of the ancient farming culture on the seasons.

谷雨*玉林

布谷不知山有雨，

看山犹是晴无恙。

栽培未必为君手，

只盼时雨丝柔长。

谷雨*桂林

雨打窗台知有味，
风吹竹林自成曲。
雨后自觉精神健，
更喜霓虹临天际。

谷雨*海口

一夜风雷起蛰龙，

千山万水尽春容。

不知何处飞来雨，

洗出人间百谷浓。

The Lixia

Lixia is the seventh solar term in the twenty-four solar terms, and the first solar term in summer. At this time, the handle of the Big Dipper points to the southeast, and the ecliptic longitude of the sun reaches 45° . The beginning of summer is an important solar term that indicates that all things are entering the peak season for growth. The almanac: "Dou refers to the southeast dimension, which is the beginning of summer. Everything has grown up here, so it is called the beginning of summer." After the beginning of summer, the sunshine increases, gradually heats up, thunderstorms increase, and crops enter a stage of vigorous growth.

立夏*三亚

烈 日 光 芒 射 斗 牛，

一 时 人 物 尽 风 流。

不 知 天 地 为 何 意，

只 有 江 山 似 旧 秋。

立夏*海口

夏日园林春色深，

东风吹绿上高阴。

不知何处飞花片，

犹带馀香入画琴。

立 夏*玉 林

夏来春去两无情，

一任东风吹雨晴。

花落不知人意懒，

鸟啼犹似客愁生。

青山有约常相对，

白发多端只自惊。

莫怪年光催短景，

The Xiaoman

Xiaoman, the eighth solar term in the twenty-four solar terms, is also the second solar term in summer. Xiaoman, fighting nails, the sun reaches 60° of the ecliptic longitude, and meets on May 20-22 of the Gregorian calendar every year. The name Xiaoman has two meanings. First, it is related to climate and precipitation. During the Xiaoman solar term, the rainstorms in the south begin to increase, and the precipitation is frequent; the folk saying goes, "the small fullness is small, the rivers are gradually full". The "full" in Xiaoman refers to the abundance of rain. Second, it is related to agricultural wheat. During the Xiaoman solar term in the northern region, there is little or no rain. This "full" does not refer to precipitation, but to the fullness of wheat.

小 满*南 宁

夏 日 园 林 小 满 时，

绿 阴 深 处 有 花 枝。

东 风 不 管 人 憔 悴，

吹 落 庭 前 一 树 棋。

小满*玉林

雨过园林绿正肥，

一帘疏影燕争围。

晚来风定无人管，

只有黄鹂自在飞。

小满*上海

绿阴深处小池塘，

满庭花影月如霜。

一阵微风送暖意，

荷叶涟涟水面香。

The awn seed

The awn seed is the ninth solar term of the twenty-four solar terms, the third solar term in summer, and the beginning of the noon month of the dry and branch calendar. Douzhisi, the ecliptic longitude of the sun reaches 75° , and it meets on June 5-7 of the Gregorian calendar every year. The meaning of "awn seed" is "grain crops with awns can be planted, but they will be invalid after this." The temperature rises significantly, the rainfall is abundant, and the air humidity is high, which is suitable for the cultivation of cereal crops such as late rice. Farming is based on the solar term of "mang seed", after which the survival rate of planting is getting lower and lower. It is the reflection of the ancient farming culture on the seasons.

芒种*乡村振兴

一路华灯照江滨，

万里风烟入目新。

莫道农家无好处，

麦苗青嫩菜花歌。

芒种*上海

雨脚如麻不暂停，

一年烈日又将至。

天风吹浪打桥头，

只有荷花似旧清。

芒种*玉林

一夜高温不可当，

天公无处著炎凉。

今朝风雨连三日，

隔江遥望云天宫。

The summer solstice

The summer solstice is the 10th solar term of the twenty-four solar terms. Dou refers to noon; the sun's yellow longitude is 90° ; the festival is on June 21-22 of the Gregorian calendar. The summer solstice is the turning point of the northward travel of the sun, after the summer solstice the point of direct sunlight begins to move southward from the Tropic of Cancer (23° 26'N). For our country located in the area north of the Tropic of Cancer, after the summer solstice, the height of the sun at noon begins to decrease day by day; for the area in our country located in the south of the Tropic of Cancer, the height of the noon sun begins to decrease day by day only after the sun returns to the south after the summer solstice.

夏至*玉林

满城红云映玉林，

国色天香两头吟。

皆知此物非凡品，

盛世造就平民心。

夏至*玉林

一袭红衣白玉身，

笑看风流千年事。

自从栽落玉林地，

却向香肉谦谦身。

夏至*玉林

荔枝熟透绿波边，

一片红云满画船。

暑气已随清流去，

闲身犹在甘回味。

The xiaoshu

Xiaoshu is the eleventh of the twenty-four solar terms, the end of the noon month and the beginning of the lunar month. Dou refers to Xin, the sun reaches 105 degrees of the ecliptic longitude and meets on July 6-8 of the Gregorian calendar every year. Shu means hot, and Xiaoshu means little heat, not very hot. Although Xiaoshu is not the hottest season of the year, it is immediately followed by the hottest solar term of the year, Dashu. Many places in my country have entered the season with the most thunderstorms since Xiaoshu.

小暑*三亚

小雨洗凉飔，

清风入翠微。

一声吹暑气，

万籁响帱旻。

小暑*玉林

夏日炎蒸不可当，

小蚊何事苦猖忙。

一时飞去无寻处，

只在青苔白石床。

小暑*玉林

赤日炙人汗欲流，

水瓜初熟绿阴凉。

一番雨过青山净，

十里风来白鸟翔。

野菜味甘宜小摘，

园蔬色美称新尝。

老夫自笑无他事，

只有诗情未尽亡。

The Great Heat

Great Heat, one of the twenty-four solar terms, the last solar term in summer. The 15th day after the minor heat is not the big heat; the ecliptic longitude of the sun is 120° ; the Gregorian calendar is July 22-24. "Shu" means hot, and Dashu means extreme heat. The big heat is relatively hotter than the small heat. It is the most sunny and hottest solar term in the year, and the "humidity and heat" reaches its peak at this time. The climate characteristics of the Great Heat: high temperature and extreme heat, frequent thunderstorms and typhoons.

The big summer solar term coincides with the "Zhongfu" in the "dog days" and is the hottest time of the year. During the big summer season, the sun is fierce, the temperature is high, humid and rainy. Although it is hard to suffer from heat and humidity, it is very beneficial to the growth of crops, and crops grow the fastest during this period.

大暑*三亚

炎风烈日昼昏冥，

大暑如焚火不停。

天地无情人易老，

江山有恨水空泠。

一声霹雳惊飞鸟，

万里乾坤失太星。

我欲乘槎问牛女，

可能相对话飘萤。

大暑*玉林

一夜狂风卷地来，

满天飞雨洗尘埃。

云连远岫青无际，

水拍长空白不开。

万里江山浑是墨，

百年身世总成灾。

何当扫尽妖氛净，

散作清凉遍八桂。

大暑*上海

炎风吹雨过前溪，

湿热交替不可期。

谁知三伏清凉地，

更有荷花似海棠。

The beginning of autumn

The beginning of autumn is the 13th solar term in the twenty-four solar terms. The change of the whole nature is a gradual process. The beginning of autumn is a turning point in which the yang qi gradually withdraws, the yin qi gradually grows, and gradually changes from yang to yin. In nature, everything begins to grow from flourishing to desolate maturity.

立秋*上海

阳气下沉而渐落，

万物随之亦萧然。

人生百岁能几日，

莫待秋风吹鬓边。

立秋*玉林

一夜西风动碧梧，
满庭凉影月模糊。
不知今日秋多少，
只有寒蝉噪画图。

立秋*上海

暑去秋来夏已深，

一年容易又侵寻。

风前落叶无人扫，

雨后残花不自禁。

老眼看书浑似梦，

壮心消酒欲成吟。

何时得遂归田计，

共醉东篱菊满林。

The end of summer

The end of summer is the fourteenth of the twenty-four solar terms. Douzhiwu (southwest); the ecliptic longitude of the sun reaches 150° ; it meets on August 22-24 of the Gregorian calendar every year. To end the summer heat, that is, "exiting the summer heat", means leaving from the heat. When it comes to the end of summer, the direct sunlight continues to move southward, the solar radiation weakens, the subtropical high also retreats southward, the temperature gradually drops, and the summer heat gradually disappears. The end of summer means the end of the sweltering heat, which is still hot, but on a downward trend.

处暑*三亚

炎天气候不胜寒,

处暑方知造化难。

莫道人间无热恼,

一杯清茗且加餐。

处暑*上海

处暑气候变化大，

昼夜之间多异哉。

风吹雨打不可奈，

日落月出何时还。

人生百年能几许，

世事万端无一裁。

但愿此身长健在，

与君同上最高台。

处暑*上海

七月中元菊正芳，
东篱把酒盼重阳。
不知天地为何世，
但觉乾坤是异乡。
万里风尘双短鬓，
十年江海一归装。
故园松竹应无恙，
莫遣秋霜上两行。

The Bailu

Bailu is the 15th solar term in the "Twenty-Four Solar Terms", the third solar term in autumn, the end of the Shen month of the stem and branch calendar and the beginning of the You month. Dou refers to Gui; the sun reaches 165 degrees of the Yellow Longitude; the festival is on September 7-9 of the Gregorian calendar. "White Dew" is an important solar term reflecting the growth of cold air in nature. As the weather gradually turns cooler, the sun is still hot during the day, but the temperature drops quickly after the evening, and the temperature difference between day and night is large.

白露*北京

秋风吹白露，

零落满庭槐。

不见黄花发，

空馀红叶开。

白露*三亚中秋

秋风白露满天涯，

万里无云月正佳。

玉兔捣药不知夜，

银河泻水空浮花。

人间此夕真堪惜，

世上何时可弃他。

欲向广寒深处望，

碧梧翠竹自成家。

白露*上海中秋

秋风吹白露，

庭树已萧骚。

客思何时尽，

乡心此夜劳。

月明千里共，

天阔一鸿高。

莫问家山路，

青云不可逃。

The autumnal equinox

The autumnal equinox is the sixteenth of the twenty-four solar terms and the fourth in autumn. Douzhiyou; the sun reaches 180° of the Yellow Longitude; it meets on September 22-24 of the Gregorian calendar every year. On the autumnal equinox, the sun is almost directly on the Earth's equator, and day and night are of equal length in all parts of the world. On the autumnal equinox, "fen" means "equal division" and "half". In addition to referring to the equal division of day and night, there is also a layer of meaning equal to the division of autumn. After the autumn equinox, the position of direct sunlight moves southward, the days in the northern hemisphere are shorter and the nights are longer, the temperature difference between day and night increases, and the temperature drops day by day.

秋分*重阳节

一声嘹唳度关山,

万里秋风落叶间。

莫向天涯悲岁月,

人生到处是家湾。

秋分*玉林

雁去秋无迹，

人归日有阴。

风高天地肃，

霜重水云深。

野旷孤烟起，

山空落叶沈。

不堪回首处，

愁绝暮江浔。

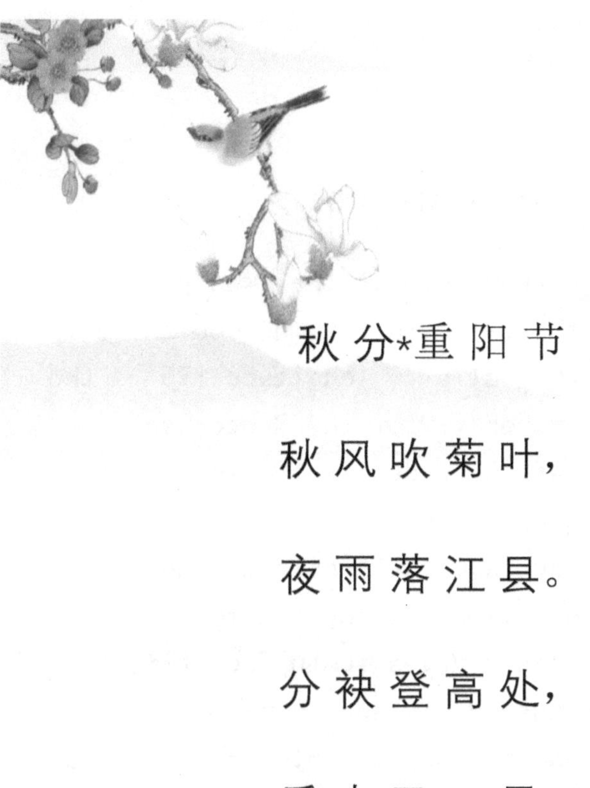

秋分*重阳节

秋风吹菊叶，

夜雨落江县。

分袂登高处，

重来又一旦。

The Cold Dew

Cold Dew is the seventeenth of the twenty-four solar terms and the fifth in autumn. Dou Zhiwu; the sun reaches the ecliptic longitude 195° ; the festival is on October 7-9 of the Gregorian calendar every year. Cold dew is the season of late autumn, the beginning of the lunar calendar. Cold Dew is a solar term that reflects the characteristics of climate change. Entering the cold dew, the cold air moves south from time to time, the temperature difference between day and night is large, and the autumn dryness is obvious.

寒露*北京

天上琼楼玉宇清，

不知何处是蓬瀛。

可怜一片冰霜色，

犹带西风万里情。

寒露*上海

有风无雨天，

一夜不见山。

云气忽变化，

万里生清寒。

我欲从之游，

浩歌发长澜。

何当驾飞鸿，

与子同跻攀。

寒露*玉林

一夜风霜露，

千山草木秋。

寒威欺客梦，

清气入诗流。

野色连云暗，

江声带雨幽。

何时重把酒，

相对话离愁。

The Frostfall

Frostfall, one of the twenty-four solar terms, is around October 23 of the Gregorian calendar every year. It means that the weather is getting colder and the first frost appears. It is the last solar term of autumn, and it also means the beginning of winter. Frostfall season is especially for health care. Important, there is a folk proverb "It is better to replenish the frost in one year", which shows the influence of this solar term on us.

霜降*玉林

寒花不自惜，

岁晚独相知。

夜里无人赏，

风前有所宜。

一枝冬色早，

万点秋阳迟。

莫作寻常看，

霜降有几时。

霜降*上海

一片冰花秋水清，

天然标格自分明。

不随桃李争春色，

独与松筠共岁成。

风动寒光摇玉影，

月移疏蕊散金英。

何人解得幽香意，

只有东篱菊正横。

霜降*玉林

秋水稻花开，

霜天万顷来。

不知何处落，

疑是故人哀。

白露沾衣冷，

黄云入望裁。

相看无限意，

独立首空徊。

The beginning of winter

The beginning of winter is the nineteenth of the twenty-four solar terms. The handle of the bucket points to the northwest, the sun's yellow longitude reaches 225°, and it meets between November 7-8 of the Gregorian calendar every year. Lidong is a seasonal solar term, indicating that winter has entered since then. Establishment is the beginning of building; winter is the end, and all things are collected. The beginning of winter means that anger begins to accumulate, and all things enter a state of recuperation and collection. Its climate also gradually changes from dry and dry in autumn to rainy and cold winter.

After the beginning of winter, the sunshine time will continue to shorten, and the height of the sun will continue to decrease at noon. Because the heat stored on the surface still has a certain amount of energy, it is generally not very cold in early winter; as time goes by, cold air activities become more frequent, and the temperature drop trend accelerates.

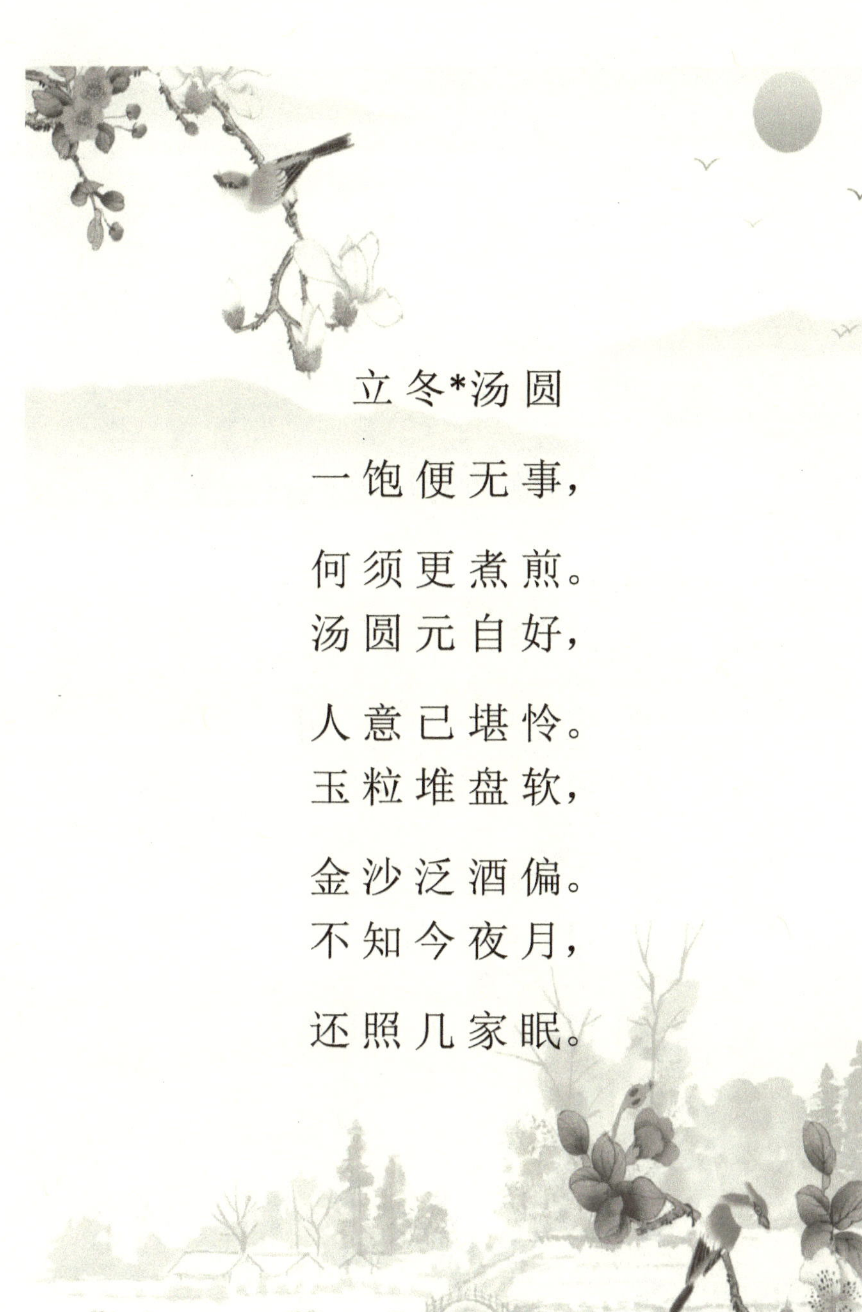

立冬*汤圆

一饱便无事，
何须更煮煎。
汤圆元自好，
人意已堪怜。
玉粒堆盘软，
金沙泛酒偏。
不知今夜月，
还照几家眠。

立冬*垂钓

寒气侵凌雪满天，
游人争渡水中船。
一身冷汗浑无力，
两眼昏花不见烟。
白鹭飞来冲钓艇，
青山围住立炊田。
此时何限伤心事，
都付渔翁理钓竿。

立冬*冬泳

不是冬泳能健康，

我们都要努力量。

身体强时须进步，

精神足处莫慌张。

一日三餐有滋味，

万事千般无险忙。

但愿人间多乐趣，

休将闲散误流光。

The Xiaoxue

Xiaoxue is the 20th solar term in the twenty-four solar terms, and the second solar term in winter. The time is on November 22 or 23 of the Gregorian calendar every year, that is, when the sun reaches the ecliptic longitude of 240° . Light snow is a solar term that reflects precipitation and temperature. It is a solar term with a high frequency of cold waves and strong cold air activities. The arrival of the light snow solar term means that the weather will get colder and precipitation will increase.

The reason why this solar term is called Xiaoxue is because "snow" is the product of cold weather. The climate during this solar term is not deep and the precipitation is not heavy. Therefore, "Xiaoxue" is used to describe the climate characteristics of this solar term. "Little snow" is a metaphor, reflecting the active cold current and increasing precipitation during this solar term, not a very small amount of snow during this solar term.

小雪*上海

腊前三日雨，

天外一宵晴。

小雪犹未落，

寒云不肯生。

风威欺酒力，

梅蕊破诗情。

莫怪频来往，

无人共此盟。

小雪*上海

小雨霏微不肯晴，

一冬寒气满沪城。

云低远岫千峰出，

雪落平田万顷成。

老树冻僵无叶立，

野梅香散有花生。

年来自笑多忧患，

独倚阑干听鸟声。

小雪*上海

昨夜雪花飞，

今朝喜气临。

不知今日瑞，

何似去年归。

The winter solstice

The winter solstice, also known as "Winter Festival" and "Hedong", is one of the twenty-four solar terms in China and one of the eight astronomical solar terms, which is opposite to the summer solstice. The winter solstice begins when the sun reaches 270° ecliptic longitude, around December 22 of the Gregorian calendar every year. According to legend, the winter solstice in the Zhou Dynasty in history was New Year's Day, which used to be a very lively day.

On the winter solstice, the position of the sun directly on the ground reaches the southernmost point of the year, almost directly on the Tropic of Capricorn (23° 26' south latitude). The northern hemisphere gets the least sunlight on this day, 50% less than the southern hemisphere. Days in the northern hemisphere are at their shortest and get shorter as you go north.

冬至*玉林

今宵冬至夜最长，

月色如银天茫迢。

东方欲明星烂漫，

西山半出云飘潇。

万里江山皆入画，

百花风雨自成潮。

明朝又是清秋候，

莫遣寒威到玉郊。

冬至*上海

雪花纷飞大地高，

万里无云天宇遥。

一夜东风吹冻解，

满城和气乐今朝。

冬至*上海

雪里梅花色，

寒来不肯春。

清香无俗韵，

幽思有馀真。

野水浮芳浪，

山云带月匀。

谁家楼上望，

应是隔年人。

The Xiaohan

Xiaohan is the twenty-third solar term in the twenty-four solar terms. It is the end of the sub-month of the dry and branch calendar and the beginning of the ugly month. For China, this is around the time of "March 9th" and Xiaohan marks the beginning of the coldest day of the year. "The Seventy-two Hours of the Moon Order": "The December festival, the cold at the beginning of the month is still small, so it is said that the half moon is big."

In ancient China, Xiaohan was divided into three stages: "One waits for Yanbei Township, two waits for magpies to start their nests, and three waits for pheasants to start robbers". The ancients believed that geese migrated along yin and yang among migratory birds. At this time, the yang qi had moved, so the geese began to move. Migrate to the north; at this time, magpies can be seen everywhere in the north, and they feel the yang energy and start to build their nests; the "robin" of the third stage "pheasant" means chirping. And tweet.

小寒*北京

冰上行人不可留，

出门一步即千愁。

风吹白草连天起，

雪压黄沙匝地流。

野店酒香沽未得，

故园山色望中幽。

何时共作江湖客，

醉把渔竿弄钓舟。

小寒*玉林

寒气弥漫不可寻，

冷风吹雪满山林。

谁知万里无冰地，

一夜飘零到玉成。

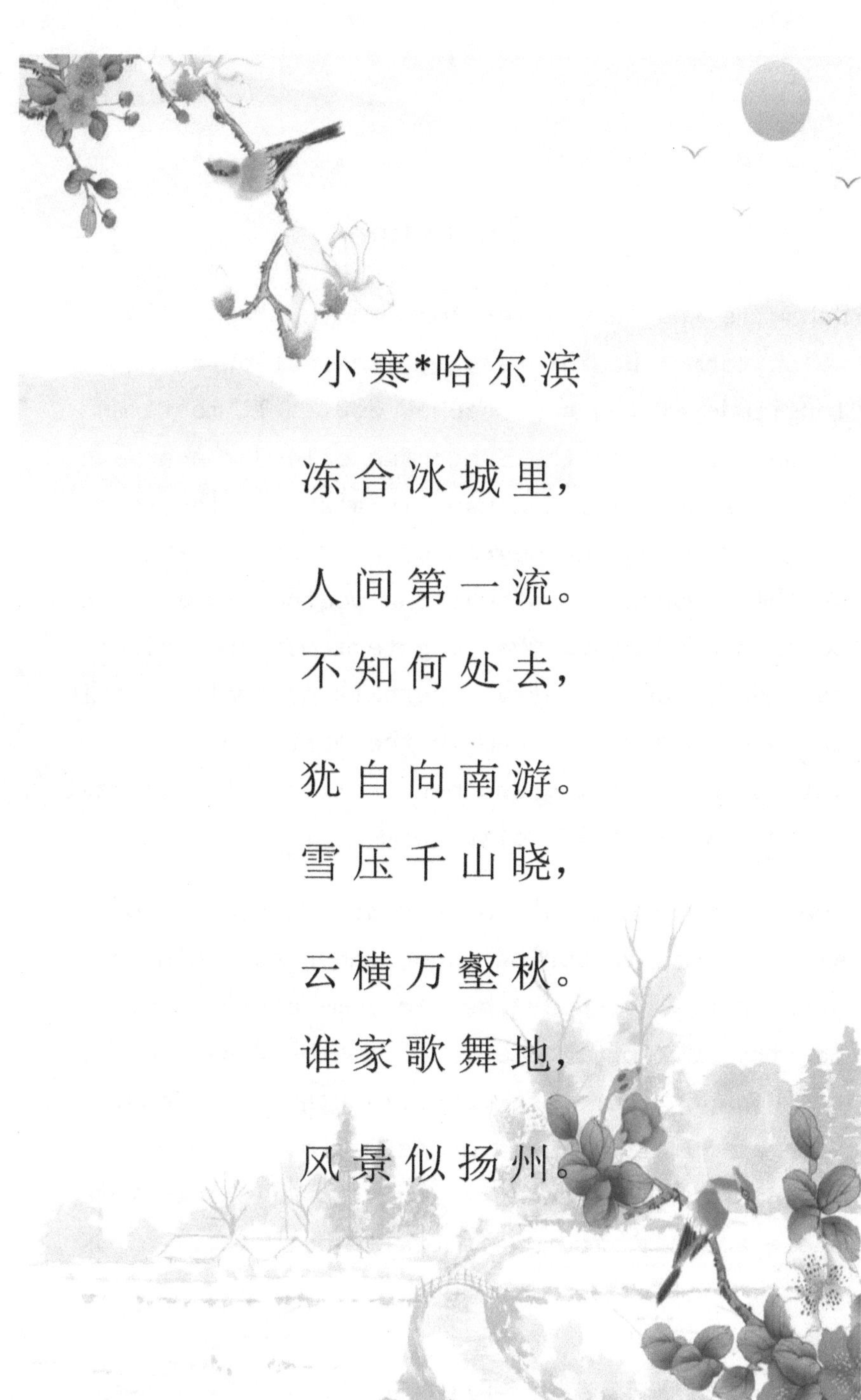

小寒*哈尔滨

冻合冰城里，

人间第一流。

不知何处去，

犹自向南游。

雪压千山晓，

云横万壑秋。

谁家歌舞地，

风景似扬州。

The Dahan

Dahan is the last solar term in the twenty-four solar terms. Douzhi is ugly; the ecliptic longitude of the sun reaches 300° ; it meets on January 20-21 of the Gregorian calendar every year. Dahan, like Xiaohan, is also a solar term that indicates the degree of coldness of the weather. Dahan means that the weather is extremely cold. According to the long-term meteorological records of our country, there is no small cold in the big cold solar term in the northern region; but for most of the southern regions, the coldest is in the big cold solar term.

The great cold is at the end of the year, and winter comes to spring. Once the great cold is over, a new cycle begins. In some parts of my country, during the period from the Great Cold to the Lichun, there are many important folk customs, such as removing the old and making new ones, making sausages, and offering sacrifices to the stove and tail teeth. The tail tooth festival, also known as "to make teeth", "to make teeth sacrifice", etc., there is a folk custom of the whole family to sit together and "eat tail teeth" after the tooth sacrifice.

大寒*上海

冻合江天雪满山，

出门一步不能攀。

何人为我传消息，

今日春风到柳间。

大寒*北京

雪里寻梅不见花，

出门闲看小儿娃。

谁知一片冰天上，

却在东风十万家。

大寒*三亚

冻云遮不尽，

春色近如何。

水浪万人渡，

山花百鸟和。

天高亚龙湾，

地阔蝴蝶谷。

欲寻仙踪迹，

南海慈悲心。

（完）

9798847830775

www.ingramcontent.com/pod-product-compliance
Lightning Source LLC
LaVergne TN
LVHW041126150826
845673LV00007B/2198

9798847830775